first quartet album

for strings

(two violins-viola-cello)

Compiled, Arranged, and Edited
by HARVEY S. WHISTLER and HERMAN A. HUMMEL

CONTENTS

Rubank

Hal•Leonard
CORPORATION
7777 W. BLUEMOUND RD. P.O. BOX 13819 MILWAUKEE, WI 53213

Andante Maestoso
from the First String Quartet

PLEYEL

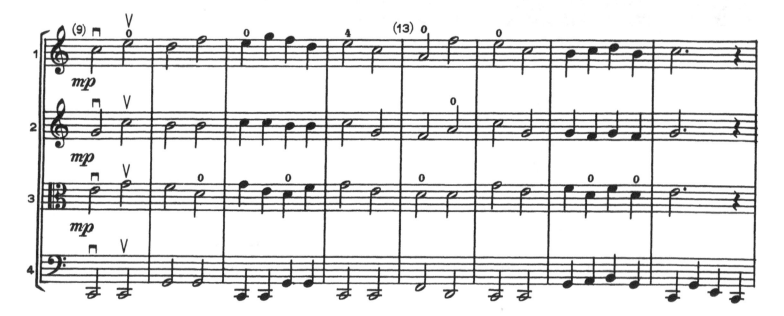

Allegro Moderato
from the Second String Quartet

PLEYEL

Deutscher Tanz

HAYDN

Der Schmetterling
(The Butterfly)

SCHUMANN

L'Alouette
(The Lark)

MENDELSSOHN

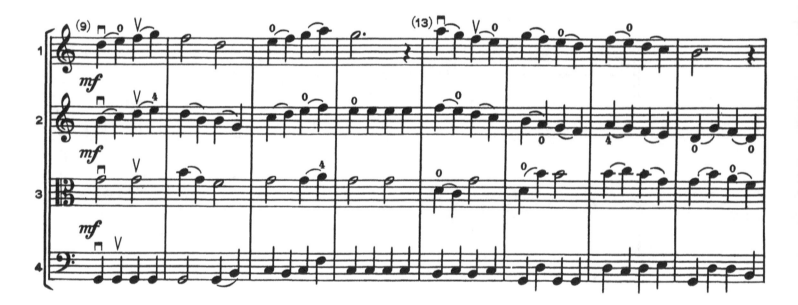

Idylle, Op. 146

DANCLA

Menuet de Concert

HAYDN

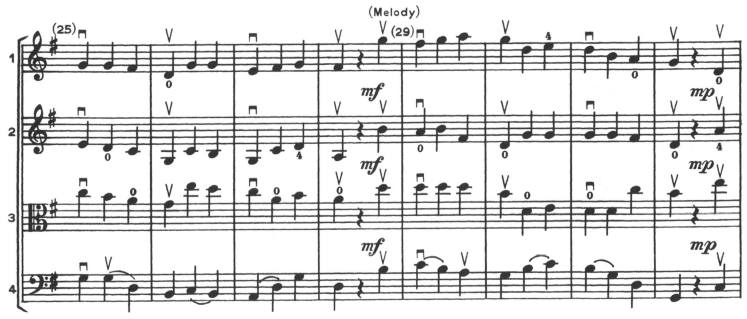
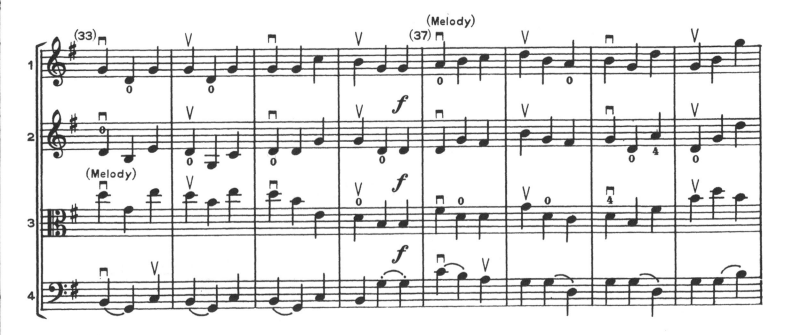
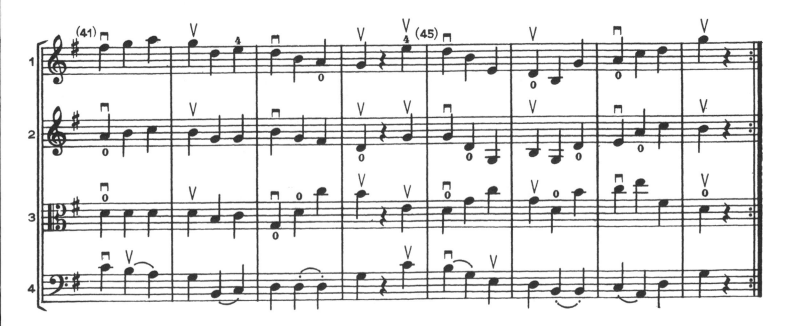

Wiegenlied
(Cradle Song)

SCHUMANN

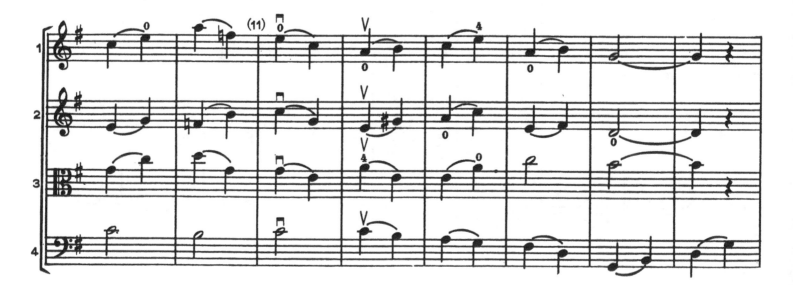

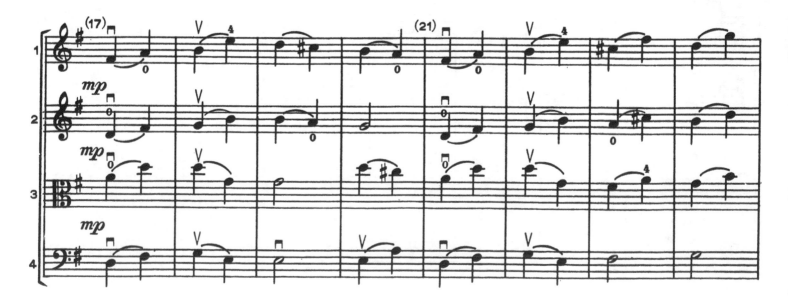

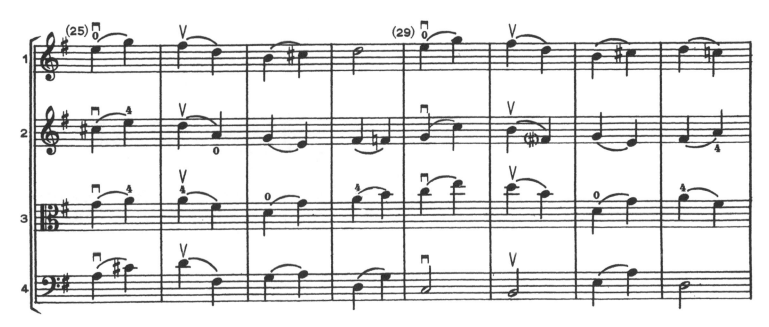

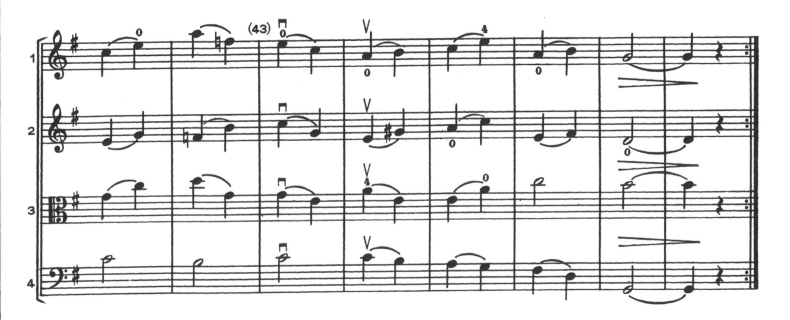

Menuet Elegante

MOZART

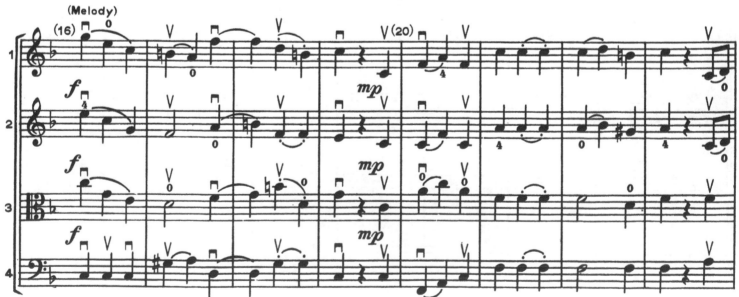

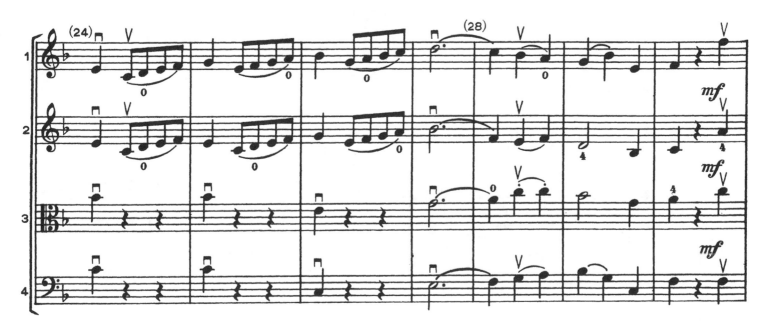

Danse Allemande

BEETHOVEN

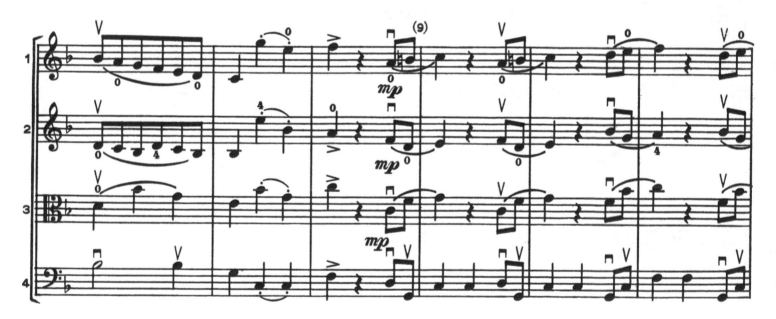

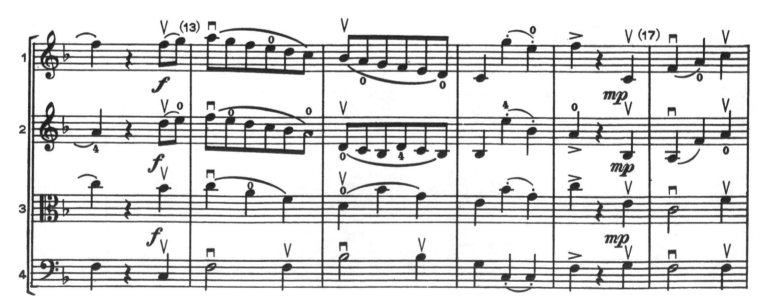

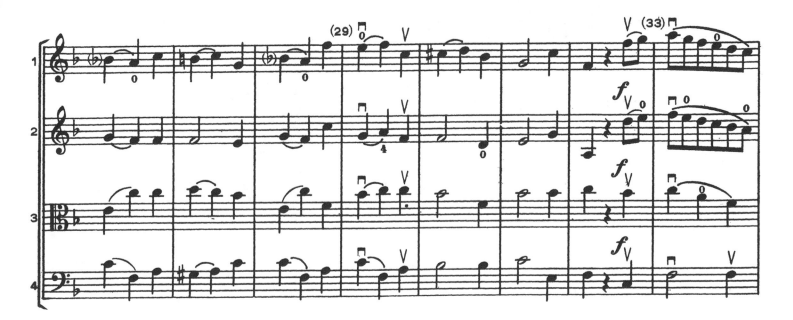

Rondino

PLEYEL

Allegretto Theme from Op. 16

BEETHOVEN

Divertissement

MOZART

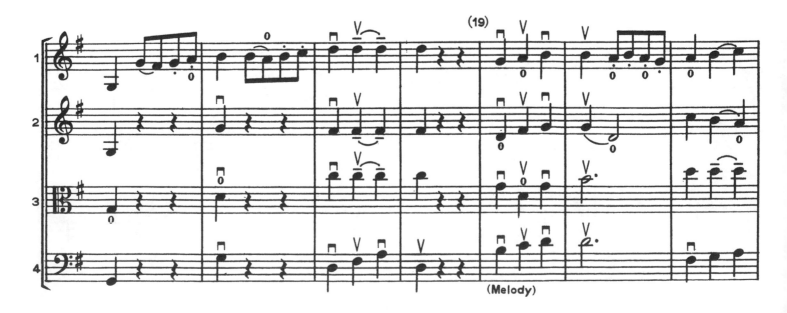

(Melody)

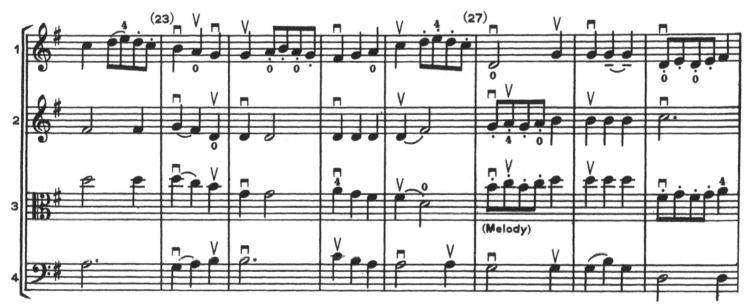

Air de Concert

HAYDN

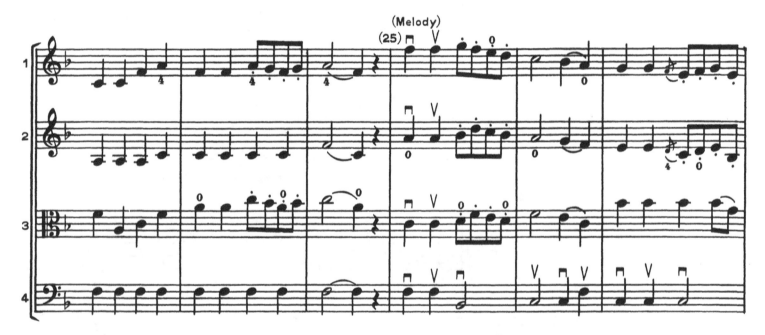

Scherzo, Op. 43

WOHLFAHRT

Theme from Allegretto Grazioso, Op. II

BEETHOVEN

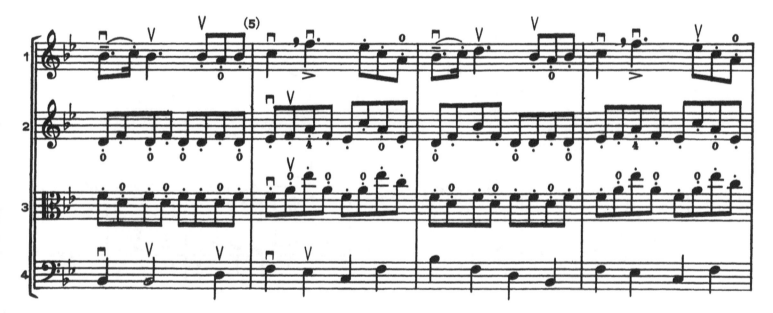

Trauermarsch from Antigone

MENDELSSOHN

Divertimento in D

BEETHOVEN

Canzonetta
from the Quartet, Op. 16

PANOFKA

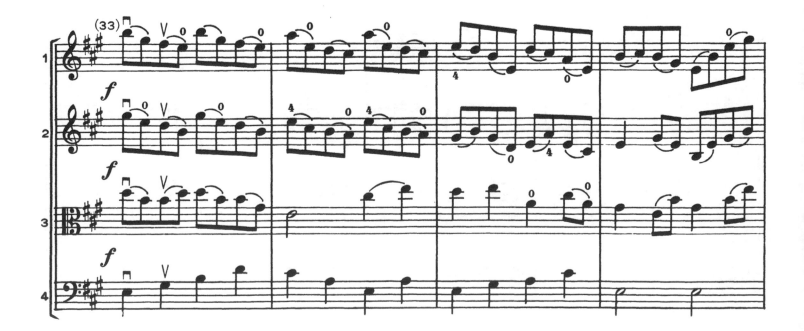

Rondo from Sonata, Op. 137, No. 1

SCHUBERT